ARAM KHACHATURIAN

DANCE NO. 1

for Violin and Piano
(1925)

ED 4147

First printing: April 2002

ISBN 978-0-634-03668-2

G. SCHIRMER, Inc.

DISTRIBUTED BY

7777 W. BLUEMOUND RD. P.O. BOX 13819 MILWAUKEE, WI 53213

Dance No. 1 (1925) for violin and piano was left unpublished during the composer's lifetime. A complete manuscript of this early composition found in the Khachaturian archives was used to prepare this edition.

The 1926 work previously published and catalogued as Dance No. 1, with the dedication to Gabrielian, should henceforth be known as "Dance."

DANCE NO. 1
for Violin and Piano

Aram Khachaturian
(1925)

Allegretto comodo

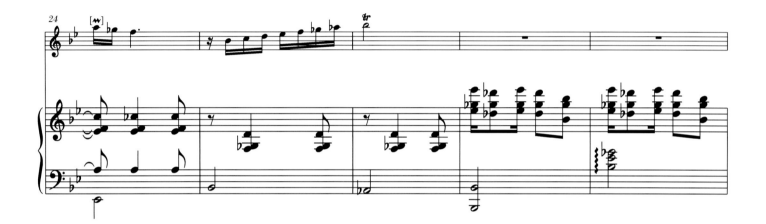

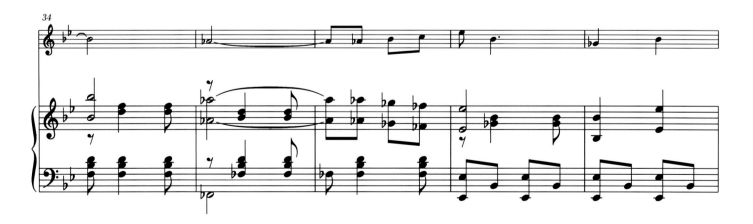

Violin

DANCE NO. 1
for Violin and Piano

Aram Khachaturian
(1925)

Allegretto comodo